THOMAS KINKADE

with Anne Christian Buchanan

Let Your Light Shine

Harvest House Publishers
Eugene, Oregon

Let Your Light Shine

Text Copyright © 2001 by Media Arts Group, Inc., Morgan Hill CA 95037
and Harvest House Publishers, Eugene OR 97402

Kinkade, Thomas, 1958-
      Let your light shine / Thomas Kinkade.
           p.cm.
      "Text ... has been excerpted from Simpler times / by Thomas Kinkade"–T.p. verso.
      ISBN 0-7369-0635-5
      1. Peace of mind. 2. Simplicity. 3. Life. 4. Quality of life. 5. Kinkade, Thomas, 1958–
      I. Kinkade, Thomas, 1958- Simpler times. II. Title.

      BF637.P3 K55 2001
      179'.9–dc21

Media Arts Group, Inc.
900 Lightpost Way
Morgan Hill, CA 95037
1.800.366.3733

Text for this book has been excerpted from *Simpler Times* by Thomas Kinkade (Harvest House Publishers, 1996).

Verses are taken from the Holy Bible, New International Version®.
Copyright © 1973, 1978, 1984 by the International Bible Society.
Used by permission of Zondervan Publishing House.

Design and production by Koechel Peterson & Associates, Minneapolis, Minnesota

You are the light of the world. A city on a hill cannot be hidden.

Neither do people light a lamp and put it under a bowl. Instead

they put it on its stand, and it gives light to everyone in the house.

In the same way, let your light shine before men, that they may

see your good deeds and praise your Father in heaven.

—MATTHEW 5:14-16

I've always loved the stars.

I love to stand out on a summer's night, far away from the lights of the city, and gaze up at all those winking points of light shining through the mysterious darkness. Thinking about all the endless miles that light has traveled. Wondering…about today and tomorrow.

When I was a child, someone told me that you can turn on a flashlight and aim it at one star, and that even after you turned the flashlight off the light would keep going—on and on, year after year, even century after century, until it eventually reached the stars.

Now I realize that concept won't hold up to any kind of scientific verification. But that image—of a tiny light shining on across the miles and through the ages—has stayed with me. It speaks to my deep desire to lead a life that matters over the long run—one that will still have an impact after I have gone.

What thou lov'st well is thy true heritage.

—EZRA POUND

Have regular hours for work and play; make each day both useful and pleasant, and prove that you understand the worth of time by employing it well. Then youth will be delightful, old age will bring few regrets, and life will become a beautiful success.

—LOUISA MAY ALCOTT

I don't think I'm unique in this feeling. I think it's a yearning built into every human spirit. We all want our light to keep going somehow. We all yearn to touch the stars.

How will we know we've succeeded? In a sense, we won't. There's nothing you or I can do to guarantee that our name or our accomplishments will be remembered here on earth. Fashions change. Memories are fickle. Cataclysms alter the face of the earth. I have no way of knowing whether a given painting will end up in a museum or be lost in a fire.

But there are some things we all can do to shine our flashlight up to the stars.

We can work to lay a legacy, to create a heritage. We can do what we do with posterity in mind. We can carry out our vocation with an intention of giving a gift to another generation.

And now these three remain: faith, hope, and love.

But the greatest of these is love.

—1 CORINTHIANS 13:13

I saw Eternity the other night,

Like a great ring of pure and endless light...

—HENRY VAUGHAN

My desire to leave a legacy is one of the reasons I've chosen to spend my life making art. Art is made to last. Most fine artists I know expect their creations to have a life beyond the next fad or the next ad campaign—preferably beyond the next generation.

In fact, nothing makes me happier than the people who buy three prints because "we have three children, and this way we can pass them on." Nothing inspires me as an artist like the thought that I may be creating heirlooms for future generations.

I am not saying my art will live forever. I have no control over earthquakes or oxidizing paint formulas or—even more fickle—artistic taste.

And yet I can still paint with the long term in mind. I can paint with an eye to universal human themes. I can strive to remain true to what I see as timeless values.

This desire to create works that stand the test of time has determined to a large degree my choice of subjects. I paint trees and mountains and gardens. I paint old, sturdy homes and cottages with warm windows that hint at family homecomings. I paint historic cities. And in all my paintings I strive for that sense of universal human longing—for home, for nature, for fellowship, for the beautiful.

What a joy it is to be able to create something. Creativity is one of the great privileges of being human.

You apply hands and mind and spirit to fashion something that did not exist before in that precise form. You touch the universe with your own unique personality and somehow at least a little corner of the universe is changed. And in the process, a part of you is created anew.

There is something deeply refreshing about any truly creative pursuit. And the benefits of creative endeavor don't depend on the quality of the endeavor. It is the very act of creating that renews you.

This is why I am so passionate about encouraging people to paint or draw—to create—regardless of whether or not they have "talent." I believe that any creative endeavor pays magnificent benefits for the time invested.

Not only does it afford the simple, childlike satisfaction of playing with materials—smearing paint, scribbling ideas and images, pounding with hammer and nails—but it also helps us make connections and understand life a little better.

Creativity is woven into the fabric of a meaningful life. And there are as many paths to creativity as there are human beings on this planet. You can be a creative homemaker and mother. (I am married to one.) You can also be a creative builder, a creative gardener, a creative hang glider. There is creativity in solving personal problems, in overcoming obstacles, in keeping relationships warm.

Light tomorrow with today.

—ELIZABETH BARRETT BROWNING

Thomas
Kinkade

I do not believe in a fate that falls on men

however they act; but I do believe in a fate

that falls on them unless they act.

—G.K. CHESTERTON

Creativity is not optional equipment. It's built-in potential, a seedling planted deep in the human personality. And like any other human possibility, creativity can be helped to grow and flourish. Because both my happiness and my livelihood depend on maintaining my own creativity, I have a vested interest in understanding it. So I have watched other people and taken note of myself, and I have reached a few conclusions.

First of all, creativity is contagious. You catch it from being around other creative people. My own creativity thrives when I expose myself to what others are doing. I love to wander through galleries and museums, to read art books and monograshps, to let myself be uplifted and inspired and humbled. I love to be around other artists, to talk together and even to paint or sketch together.

Remember that you are an actor in a drama, of such a part as it may please the master to assign you, for a long time or for a little as he may choose. And if he will you to take the part of a poor man, or a cripple, or a ruler, or a private citizen, then you may act that part with grace! For to act well the part that is allotted to us, that is indeed ours to do, but to choose it is another's.

—EPICTETUS

Thomas Kinkade

And if anyone gives even a cup of cold water to one of these little ones because he is my disciple, I tell you the truth, he will certainly not lose his reward.

—MATTHEW 10:42

But exposure to creativity is much more than just talking shop with people who share the same endeavor. I find that my creativity as an artist soars through exposure to many different kinds of endeavors. I love to read — everything from fine literature to pop culture. I listen to books on tape while I paint. I pore through volumes of romantic poetry, through twentieth-century adventure novels. I collect popular literature from the 1930s, 1940s, and 1950s — dime novels, pulp magazines, and advertising. I browse antique shops, go to movies, attend meetings with creative people in the company that publishes my prints. And of course I make plenty of time to get out in nature, to let myself be inspired and renewed by contact with the work of the Creator.

Creativity is contagious, but that's just the beginning of the process. Motivation needs to turn to ideas, and ideas need to be incubated. You need to move things around in your head and with your hands. You experiment. You move your mind around, allowing yourself to look at what you're doing from different angles.

Thomas Kinkade

One of my most helpful creative tools is an idea board in my study. On it I post notes, sketches, fragments of thoughts, ideas, verses, cartoons—whatever has stirred my imagination in recent days. And then, whenever I pass by, I look over the board and rearrange the items. Because I am a very visual person, this process seems to stir the pot of my creativity, encouraging me to think in fresh ways.

And contrary to much popular wisdom, I have found that all of this happens best in a structured environment. Creativity flourishes under a gentle routine. It delights in an unhurried atmosphere. It requires feeding and nurturing, but not constant stimulation and "enrichment." And it is not so easily stifled as some people would have you think.

Rules, for example, don't stifle creativity—at least not in themselves. Creativity can blossom within a structure, just as tomato plants thrive in their cages and roses bloom on their trellises.

Let a man in a garret but burn with enough

tenacity and he will set fire to the whole world.

—ANTOINE DE SAINT-EXUPERY

The future belongs to those who live

in the beauty of the dream.

—ELEANOR ROOSEVELT

Repetitive routines don't necessarily stifle creativity either. Some of my best ideas have come while I sat for hours signing my name to prints. Shelling peas, walking to the store, any kind of "mindless" physical routine can provide a valuable backdrop for the creative mind to work. In fact, I find that the simple, routine act of walking is a wonderful stimulus to creative thinking.

Up to a point, deprivation doesn't even stifle creativity. In fact, imaginations often soar in very simple or even bare environments. Some of the world's greatest art and literature has come from men and women who knew deprivation. And even people with no professional background in art have demonstrated remarkable ingenuity in constructing a life out of the materials at hand—as evidenced by patchwork quilts and cantilevered barns and carved wooden animals and other examples of frontier handiwork.

Our creativity will become our prayer, born of simple attention to what is around, and enhancing the world by its expression.

—ELIZABETH J. CANHAM

I grew up in a very simple, unembellished environment, in a small town where I often felt starved for experience. But my brother and I were always inventing mysteries, making up stories to act out, building tree forts and networks of tunnels in the high grass. And of course I had lots of time to be outside, to ride my bike, to wander around with my sketchbook and draw. My creativity was not hampered in the least by my relative lack of "enriching" activities.

To be creative, all you need is room to play, room to think, room to just be.

The desire for longevity as an artist also helps me resist the temptation to hurry my work along, to cut corners, to think in terms of productivity rather than quality. I always try to remember what someone once told me: "They'll forget how quickly you do it, but they'll always remember how well you do it." And so I try to give each painting its due. I am willing to put in the hours I need to put in.

And yet that same desire to live for the long term tells me that my work cannot be my ultimate priority. The things we make cannot be our most important legacy.

*Creativeness in the
world is, as it were,
the eighth day of creation.*

—NICOLAS BERDYAEV

I put my heart and my soul into my paintings, but in the long term they are still only flat pieces of canvas with daubs of color covering them. They are only material objects, just as the Empire State Building and the pyramids and the earth itself are material objects. Even these long-lasting things are not eternal.

My most important legacy, the one that can carry my little light onward toward the stars, will be the contribution I make to the lives of other human beings—because my faith in God affirms that human souls are the only things in this life that continue forever. Material things are subject to moth and rust and death, but according to the Bible, human souls are eternal. And therefore my true heritage must be my loving contribution to other human souls.

That belief and my personal Christian faith keeps my family at the top of my list of priorities, because my family members are the human beings I touch most often and most deeply. After all, if my wife and my children are eternal beings, then the way I treat them will have eternal consequences. This, even more than my paintings, will keep my light shining and help me reach the stars.

And this principle extends even beyond my family. In giving to other humans, in serving them, in helping them, I have the opportunity to affect their eternal destiny. In service, therefore, lies my chance to touch the stars.

I've seen this reality echo and re-echo in the life of my mother, who has invested her life in the service of her fellow humans. To my brother and sister and me, she donated her energy, her care, her passion for art and literature, and her fierce determination to march to the beat of a different drummer. To the people she serves in the soup kitchen sponsored by her local church, she donates her concern and her compassion. And that, to me, is her most lasting legacy.

I am convinced this is true for every human being, regardless of faith, background, occupation, or circumstance. When I am loving today, I am sending out my light to touch tomorrow's stars.

But that brings us to a paradox, a mystery of time and eternity. Simply put: We can aim for the eternal, but we can act only in the present moment.

Keep on loving each other as brothers.

—HEBREWS 13:1

We can work at establishing a legacy for tomorrow, but we can do this successfully only when we are living fully today. It's what I'm doing right now with my flashlight that determines whether the light will keep on going throughout the generations.

This reality is, to me, the key to a full yet purposeful life. As a Christian and a man of prayer, it is what enables me to experience the present joyfully and passionately, yet still make plans for the future. It is the reality that reminds me that stopping to examine that bug with my daughters may pay longer-term dividends than rushing to my studio to finish a painting.

Our best chance of touching, in our own small way, the eternal is to live the life we're given, savoring the now, deciding for the future, remembering always that the secrets of the stars are folded tightly into the mysterious center of this present moment.

They unfold in the form of grace for where we are, purpose for where we're going, a joyous sense of enjoying the journey.

They unfold into the kind of life that's worth living.

Thomas Kinkade

Look at the stars! look, look up at the skies!

O look at all the fire-folk sitting in the air!

The bright boroughs, the circle-citadels there!

—GERARD MANLEY HOPKINS